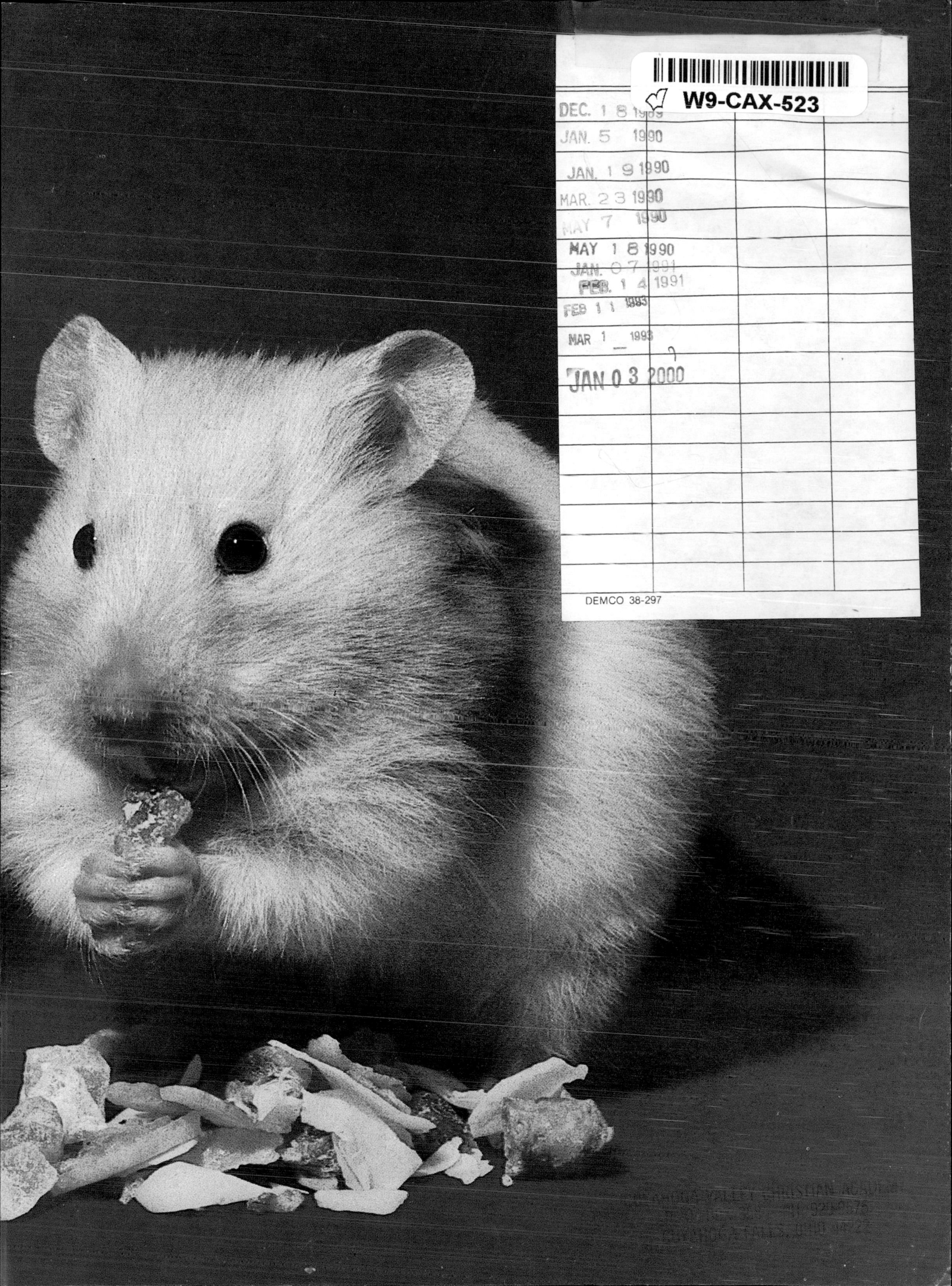

Contents

Front cover: Today there are millions of hamsters giving affection and amusement to their owners. Endpapers: One of the hamster's favorite pastimes is to store food in its cheek pouches, then deposit the hoard in a special hiding place.

Photography

Dr. Herbert R. Axelrod: 6, 8, 10, 12, 17, 20, 22, 24, 26, 29 (top), 30, 32, 38, 62, 70, 71, 72, 73, 74, 75, 77. Michael Gilroy: 9, 11, 13, 15, 18, 19, 21, 23, 25, 27, 29 (bottom), 31, 33, 34-35, 37, 39, 41, 43, 46, 47 (bottom), 49, 50, 51, 53, 56, 57, 59, 60, 61, 65, 67, 69. R. Hanson: 46. Mervin F. Roberts: 52. Cover and endpapers by Michael Gilroy.

© 1981 by TFH Publications, Inc. Ltd.

t.f.h.

ISBN 0-87666-848-1

Distributed in the U.S. by T.F.H. Publications, Inc., 211 West Sylvania Avenue, PO Box 427, Neptune, NJ 07753; in England by T.F.H. (Gt. Britain) Ltd., 13 Nutley Lane, Reigate, Surrey; in Canada to the pet trade by Rolf C. Hagen Ltd., 3225 Sartelon Street, Montreal 382, Quebec; in Canada to the book trade by H & L Pet Supplies, Inc., 27 Kingston Crescent, Kitchener, Ontario N28 2T6; in Southeast Asia by Y.W. Ong, 9 Lorong 36 Geylang, Singapore 14; in Australia and the South Pacific by Pet Imports Pty. Ltd., P.O. Box 149, Brookvale 2100, N.S.W. Australia; in South Africa by Valid Agencies, P.O. Box 51901, Randburg 2125 South Africa. Published by T.F.H. Publications, Inc., Ltd., the British Crown Colony of Hong Kong.

The T.F.H. Book of
HAMSTERS

t.f.h.

MERVIN F. ROBERTS

Hamsters In General

Many books about pets start with an apology of some sort. Your parakeet (they say) is really a budgerigar. A guinea pig is not a pig from Guinea but a cavy. A pet chameleon is actually an anole. An alligator is probably a caiman. And don't be surprised, you're told, if some rabbits are really hares.

But here is a book about a hamster, which is exactly and precisely a hamster. It has a perfectly legitimate Latin name—*Mesocricetus auratus*—but even the scientists just call it a hamster.

Originally—before selective breeding produced a greater variety in color and hair length—all pet hamsters were roughly golden in color. A majority still are, with soft, short golden-red fur over their backs and sides and darker marks—"flashes"—on their foreheads and cheeks, and with bellies bluish-gray to white.

A hamster's eyes are bright and bold and curious, but its eyesight is not keen.

The hamster's skin is very loose on its body (it can be pulled over an inch from almost every part of the body). Eyes are bright and bold and curious, but eyesight is not keen. The feet are good at grasping. The tail is merely a stump, about one-quarter of an inch long; in fact a male of the longhaired variety generally has his tail completely hidden by his long hair.

An unusual feature of hamsters, setting them apart from most other animals, is the cheek pouch, which is used for gathering food and litter for nests and for preparing the nest litter. The pouches extend from the cheeks to the shoulder and can hold food approximately equal to one-half of the animal's volume. The inside is a soft tissue which slightly moistens the material being stored. The pouches do not really stand out except when they are full and the animal is viewed from above.

The story of the golden hamster as a pet began in 1930, when Professor I. Aharoni of the Department of Zoology of Hebrew University, Jerusalem, acquired an adult female and her litter of twelve babies near Aleppo, Syria. A few months afterward, he gave one male and two females of the wild litter to the university, and there Dr. Ben-Menahem first bred them. This trio is believed to be the source of every living hamster today. Some of the young were sent to England in 1931, and from there a few were shipped to the United States Public Health Service Research at Carville, Louisiana, where they were used for medical research.

It was the research scientists who first noticed that hamsters made fine pets, and it was probably from the stock at Carville that hamsters became available to the public. By now there are certainly more hamsters in captivity than there are in all the hamster burrows in Syria.

It was the research scientist who first noticed that hamsters made fine pets. Right: The white rings or "spectacles" around the eyes give this hamster its name, spectacled hamster. Below: This species, the Chinese hamster, is smaller than the normal golden hamster most commonly found in pet shops today. Its tail is longer also.

WHY HAVE A HAMSTER AS A PET ?

Today there are millions of hamsters giving affection and amusement to their owners. The fact that they are easy to care for, gentle, attractive and very entertaining makes them especially suitable as pets in small quarters.

Hamsters are small animals; which means that they can be comfortable in relatively small quarters—which in turn means that people who are beginning with hamsters don't have to make a large cash outlay for the hamsters' housing. Pet shops sell a wide variety of good but inexpensive hamster accommodations.

A hamster is a cuddly, hand-holdable pet. It is larger than a mouse and has a prettier face. And it doesn't have the musky odor of a male mouse.

Hamsters are amusing animals. They sit up, stand on their hind legs, sit like bears and climb and grasp practically anything they can get their "hands" on. They can grasp with their hind feet as well, and they enjoy doing acrobatic tricks.

Hamsters are gentle, clean, odorless and practically mute. They won't utter annoying noises.

While most pets need daily care, hamsters can be left alone over a weekend if necessary, because they hoard food and don't drink much.

Hamsters' hoarding habit makes them especially interesting to watch. (The name hamster, incidentally, comes from the German *hamstern,* meaning "to hoard.") You will be fascinated as you watch a hamster stuff food into its enormous cheek pouches and then take it out and hide it "for a rainy day."

Hamsters are handsome little animals, and they come in several colors and textures; they also come in shorthaired and longhaired forms.

Hamsters are hardy and easy to breed. And talk about speedy! They are unique in their ability to reproduce themselves only sixteen days after mating. So, if you want a family of them, or if you're thinking of unusual presents for your friends and relatives, you need not wait long.

Their life span is about 1000 days maximum, so if you get tired of keeping hamsters, just stop breeding them and in less than three years you will be free. And a bit lonely.

They enjoy being hand-fed, played with and fondled. Their fur is soft and pleasant to touch. If one escapes, it will probably be happy to return to its cage.

Grooming is a cinch. Their teeth and nails generally wear down as they grow and need no attention. There's no reason to bathe a hamster (isn't that a relief!); it will groom itself clean as long as it's healthy. Even the coat of the longhaired variety needs only an occasional gentle brushing.

A hamster is a cuddly, hand-holdable pet.

Hamsters enjoy being hand-fed, played with and fondled.

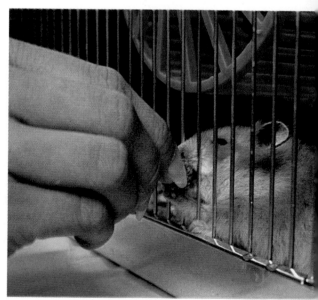

This black-eyed white hamster is busy grooming itself. There's no reason to bathe a hamster.

How To Choose A Hamster

A few minutes of observation of hamsters in a pet shop will probably convince you that it would be fun to own one. The next step is to choose the one for you.

AGE

It is best to get your hamster just a few weeks after it has been weaned away from its mother—at about five weeks of age. Luckily, however, the hamster is so gentle and so easily tamed that even a year-old animal can be trained without too much difficulty. But there's another good reason for choosing a baby, if you're being really practical. Since hamsters live only about a thousand days and cost as little as they do, you can figure that a year-old hamster has already lived out a chunk of your investment. On the other hand, a hamster younger than thirty days is too young to move, too young to play with and too young to have good control of its emotions or its locomotion. Baby hamsters have poor vision, and those under thirty days will have a great deal of trouble seeing things—the edge of a table, for instance. While older hamsters will come to the edge of a table and stop, the baby will often go right over the edge and topple to the floor. This is dangerous because, unlike mice, hamsters don't seem to be able to flip about in the air and fall lightly on their feet.

SEX

Your hamster can be of either sex, since both males and females make good pets. A pair could make thousands of good pets. A word of warning, though: don't buy a pair unless you know in advance what you are going to do with the babies. Pet shops can probably obtain exactly what the market calls for, when there is a demand, more readily from commercial breeders than from individuals such as you. Don't plan to make your pets pay for themselves.

Male hamsters often seem to be more even-tempered and friendly than females; this may be due to the female's sensitivity during pregnancy and her negative reaction to having her newborn pups molested.

Among the longhairs the male seems to have the *slightly* longer coat.

Mature males have one or two black dots over their hips under the fur. Each is about as large as the hamster's eye and about two or three times the thickness of the skin. These marks are quite normal. They are called dimorphic pigment spots and are much like "beauty marks" in humans. Some perfectly healthy

Opposite: A satin golden hamster (at left) and a golden tortoiseshell hamster (at right).

A few minutes of observation of hamsters in a pet shop will probably convince you that it would be fun to own one.

Opposite: A light grey angora hamster—one of the longhaired variety.

hamsters will lick these spots in warm weather. Large lumps, boils, abscesses and pimples are another matter, of course.

APPEARANCE

The size of your pet when you buy it is primarily dependent on its age. However, it should weigh fifty four grams (about an ounce and a half) or more. A hamster smaller than that will have the same trouble as a very young one. The shape and general appearance of the hamster you choose is very important. Lumps, bumps, discoloration, loose hair, wet bottom or tail, stuffed or running nose, running eyes, blood anywhere and bad disposition are all symptoms which should stop you from making a purchase. Don't buy anything but a perfectly healthy pet! Then you can look forward to keeping it free from disease for the next thousand days or so. The signs of good health are soft, silken fur, plump body, a general feeling of solidity to the body, prominent bright eyes and an alert inquisitiveness.

A tiny nick or hole on a hamster's ear may be a breeder's mark, or it may be the result of a bite from a cagemate. It is not a disease, and unless you plan to exhibit your pet in a competitive show you can ignore it.

The hamster you choose should have a gentle disposition. If it is nasty and doesn't allow you to pick it up, don't buy it.

When purchasing a pet hamster, look for these signs of good health: a solid body, soft fur, large bright eyes, and an alert disposition.

VARIETIES

Hamsters today are bred in several different colors. Among the common colors are the albino, which is white with pink eyes; the pied, harlequin or panda, which are all spotted brown or beige on white with dark eyes; and a cream or beige or fawn variety with brown or ruby eyes. This latter type has several names—which are given by individual breeders but have not yet been established by common use.

Longhaired hamsters tend to cost more than short-hairs. They tend to be a bit less prolific.

Pink-eyed hamsters may have poorer vision than dark-eyed varieties. *Some* pink-eyed hamsters are known to be blind or nearly blind, but since most white hamsters are not pink-eyed but rather ruby-eyed, the problem is not as prevalent as one might suppose.

Of all of them, the most hardy is the ordinary golden (or "Syrian") variety.

The hamster you choose should have a gentle disposition. If it is nasty and doesn't allow you to pick it up, don't buy it.

PRICE

Be prepared to pay a respectable price for your pet. A hamster that costs *too* little is not really a bargain.

Besides the normal golden color, there are a variety of other colors (such as the longhaired roan male above, and the light grey tortoiseshell below) which can be obtained through successful controlled breeding.

Your hamster should come from a reputable local pet shop. Operators of such shops know their sources of supply, so they sell only healthy animals. A variety/discount store is the worst place to buy a hamster. The help is usually uninformed, the management is usually uninterested, and the livestock usually is of uncertain quality.

HAMSTER BEHAVIOR

Your pet hamster wants to explore, to play, to hide, to hoard food, to keep clean with fresh bedding and to be handled gently. Once you understand your hamster's habits, training will be easy, and you'll have a pet you can really enjoy.

First of all, hamsters like privacy—privacy from humans and also privacy from *all* other animals and *most* other hamsters. A few young specimens of the same sex do well together, but an adult female will sometimes kill a male who is introduced into her cage when she is not receptive. If you plan to keep several hamsters together in one cage, provide plenty of room, with separate nest boxes or other hiding places. Keep the sexes separate, and watch the hamsters for signs of fighting. If they do fight, separate them immediately.

Allow your hamster to get used to you before you pick it up. As you and your pet become more accustomed to one another, you may find that it is perfectly all right to reach into the cage, but don't do it the first day. When you pick up your hamster, lift his body gently. Don't grasp him by the skin or tail or leg or around the neck. Let it climb into your hand.

Hamsters are nocturnal animals, sleeping during the day. They do not like sunlight or any bright light. However, if you want to play with your hamster during the day it will not object if you awaken it gently and keep it out of the bright light until it is thoroughly awake. Don't breathe heavily or blow on your hamster. A warning sign is when your hamster's ears are curled or laid back. This often happens when you first waken it or when you disturb a mother hamster. Be patient, and soon the ears will open out and stand erect. Then you can feel reasonably sure that your pet isn't mad at you. Hamsters are naturally friendly with humans, and you will get along well by acting thoughtful and humane.

Baby hamsters are not "housebroken." They soil the cage anywhere, but since they are clean animals, by the time they are about two months old their good habits will be well established.

Hamsters have a strong feeling about what is theirs. This applies to their hoards, their homes and their babies. A pet hamster might nip its owner's hand if the

14

Once the hamster has become accustomed to being touched and handled by its owner it should be lifted by having its body cradled in the hands rather than grasped by the loose skin on the neck as shown above.

Hamsters have a strong feeling about what is theirs, as depicted by two females, a grey dominant spot and a cinnamon dominant spot (above) and a longhaired red-eyed cream hamster (below).

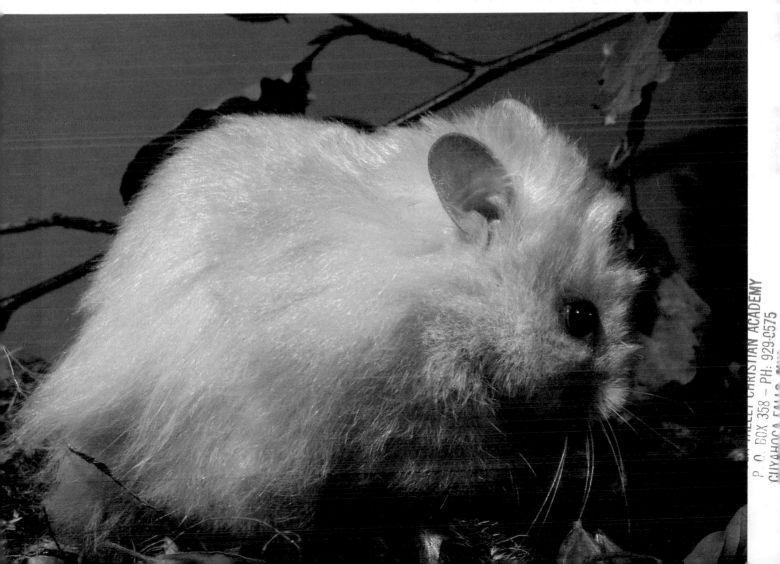

hand is thrust into the hamster's nest or even into its cage, but the same animal will be perfectly safe and tame and friendly if it is outside the cage. Sometimes females have a stronger desire to accumulate and hoard food and nesting materials than males. Male hamsters live alone and do not join in any family affairs. The male may, in fact, destroy the young, or he may be destroyed himself by the female if he ventures near the babies.

This is extremely important: A pregnant female or a new mother should be left strictly alone until the babies' eyes are open—when they are about 16 days old. Here's why:

The hamster's eyesight is not especially good, but its senses of hearing and smell are acute; in fact, like other rodents, hamsters are very smell-oriented. In a non-scientific yet practical sense their "brain" is in their nose. Your strongly non-hamster odor interferes with the familiar smell of the litter and greatly disorients the mother. Many mothers have killed or deserted their litters because the pet owner didn't know this or didn't have the patience and strength of character to leave the hamsters alone at this time. Of course the first few days are the most crucial, and as time goes on the mother becomes more tolerant.

Hamsters replace their fur about every three months. As they grow old there is a tendency for less hair to appear on the ears, until at last the ears appear quite shiny.

Hamsters hibernate, especially if the air is both moist and cold. If you keep your pet in a cage out of doors, provide a draft-free sleeping area which it can arrange to suit itself during its period of hibernation.

There is a possibility that the life span of the hamster is connected with the amount of hibernation. A hamster that hibernates two months a year may live longer than the 1000 days usually allotted. This is a field that would benefit from study by serious pet keepers.

An aquarium or bird-cage would be a suitable home for your hamster. You may prefer, however, to purchase a cage especially made for small rodents.

Housing

In general, buy, don't build. The thrill of personal accomplishment is wonderful indeed, but unfortunately anything you can build can be bought for less, and it might very well be better. You may probably build no more than a handful of hamster cages in your lifetime, but a cage manufacturer produces thousands and probably has worked out bugs you never thought of.

For large-scale breeding try stainless steel or plastic boxes with 3/8 inch wire mesh covers. For a small scale home hobby, consider an aquarium, or a birdcage, or a cage especially for small rodents available at your pet shop.

Avoid a cage having a wooden bottom. The wood will soak up the urine and will always be damp and smelly. Plastic, glass or stainless steel are all good cagebottom materials. Another reason for not recommending wood as a cage material is that it can be gnawed. If the wood is splintery and sharp it can hurt the hamster's mouth or check pouches. If it is thin, you may have an escape to contend with.

Try for something strong and simple. Remember there must be an access for water. A water dish will not work, as your hamster will quickly and deliberately fill it with bedding or feces. Hamsters are desert animals—they drink drops of dew hanging from plants, but standing water is foreign to their way of life. Don't try to change them. Remember that a hamster is a granivorous desert rodent—what little water it needs should be clean, fresh and dew-like. The water access is best handled with a bottle, rubber stopper and glass tube—from above.

The cover should latch. Not gadgety—but simple and strong and easy to lock. As escape artists, hamsters are rivaled only by snakes, monkeys and parrots.

The cover might well provide ventilation. If the cover is coarsely screened it will also be attractive to the hamster for exercise. The hamster will climb about, upside down, for hours, every night. The wire will also get its share of gnawing, which is nothing more than teeth-sharpening and release of nervous tension.

An exercise wheel is great if you can find room for it and don't mind the squeaking of the bearings all through the night.

Check your local pet shop for all your hamster's needs.

ACCESSORIES

An exercise wheel is great if you can find room for it and don't mind the squeaking of the bearings all through the night. Never during the day—only at night! There may be a silent exercise wheel—find it if you can. Hamsters *do* need to exercise; if they don't, they are subject to paralysis.

Hamsters love to play. Here's one in a playball.

This is one type of metal cage, equipped with an exercise wheel. Metal, unlike wood, will withstand the hamster's constant gnawing.

A light chocolate hamster playing in the wheel—a great form of entertainment!

One accessory for the cage is a plastic, glass or metal scoop. It should be a little larger than your largest hamster. Use it to transfer a female to the cage of the male for breeding. There are two good reasons for this. First, there is less chance of your being bitten. Remember, your hand is hamster size and it is invading another hamster's castle. Second, a female should smell like a female; she should not smell like your hand when she is introduced to the male. Perhaps your scoop can be a kitchen utensil, the kind some cooks use for dipping into flour or sugar. Another way to create a handy scoop is by cutting off the bottom and part of one side of a plastic bottle.

When you clean cages, don't use insect sprays or dusts since some may be dangerous to your animals, and if you provide 100% fresh clean bedding, the insects and insect eggs will be kept under control or entirely eliminated without the need for insecticides. This is not really a problem if you keep fewer than a hundred animals and don't introduce new stock directly "off-the-street."

If you expect to introduce additional hamsters to your stock, one or two cages should be kept empty and apart—in another room if possible—as quarantine for new or sick animals.

The cage should have a secluded area for sleeping and hoarding, and enough space for "toilet facilities" away from the sleeping and hoarding areas. It should have water, draft-free ventilation, and dry, warm cage litter. Wood shavings are best, but torn up newspaper can also be used. Keep the cage away from sunlight or any bright, glaring light. An average temperature of 68° F. is fine.

Unhappy hamsters are usually those that are crowded, not permitted seclusion, deprived of a place to hoard food, or abused by their cagemates. However, even if your hamster has a comfortable home, he may try to escape. This is only the result of his natural curiosity.

BEDDING

Weaned hamsters develop toilet habits with a little help from you. The urine is the problem, since the droppings tend to dry out quickly, and dry droppings are virtually odorless. Here is where you can help.

Provide plenty of bedding which your hamster can move around the cage. It will hide food in certain areas, build its nest elsewhere and sweep clean the spot where it leaves its liquid wastes. As the wastes evaporate, you can scrape up the remainder and then blot up the last traces with a small wad of bedding which should then be thrown away.

An assortment of hamster toys are available at your local pet shop.

The cage should have a secluded area for sleeping and hoarding, and enough space for "toilet facilities" away from the sleeping and hoarding areas. It should have water, draft-free ventilation, and dry, warm cage litter.

Keep the cage away from direct sunlight or any bright, glaring light. An average temperature of 68°F is fine.

Clean the cage often enough to keep the urine spot localized. If the *entire* cage is dirty or damp, the animal will have no cause to choose a particular spot to wet. How often? Once every week or two is good point. If you clean the cage too frequently, you will waste food and disturb the hamster's sense of security by ruining the nest and the hoard.

Remember to clean the cage of a female *while* she is being mated. She will be too busy to be bothered by your housecleaning. This technique will permit her to establish a nursery in anticipation of delivering a litter two weeks hence. Don't touch her cage contents again until the young are weaned. Since this whole process will take a month or so, it will be a good idea to provide extra bedding in this instance.

Bedding can be nearly anything which is not poisonous, overly aromatic, sharp or entangling. Paper confetti, wood chips, sawdust, shavings, mowed hay, chopped hay, cotton waste, have all been used successfully. Mr. Richard Smith of Stonehill Farms, Groton, Connecticut buys aspen wood shavings, even though he could get for free all the hay or sawdust he could possibly use. Aspen, a type of poplar, is a soft wood—it is not aromatic like cedar, nor is it full of pitch like some of the pines. Two heaping handfuls provide a two-week supply for an adult and several youngsters together in a cage.

A longhaired hamster might get its hair tangled in the wood shavings, but with a dry toothbrush you can eliminate the tangles before they become a problem.

Should you decide to go away on vacation, or should it become necessary to make a trip to the veterinarian, you'll find that most hamster cages are portable.

ESCAPES AND CAPTURES

The hamster spends a great deal of his time plotting and figuring out ways to escape. He gnaws, digs, scratches, pushes and gnaws some more. And he waits. But at least once he will find his way out, and that's that.

Escapes are a problem several ways. New Mexico has a climate like Syria—you have no business establishing, even by accident, an exotic rodent where he might take over from resident species. Another problem is that an escaped hamster might pick up parasites, ticks, fleas or disease and then when you capture him and put him back in the colony, you have introduced an open Pandora's box. Still another is the possibility of loss to a predator; to a dog, a cat or a rat a hamster is fair and likely game. Unfortunately, unlike a squirrel or hare, a hamster can't run fast enough to escape them.

The chances of finding a hamster under the ottoman, in the broom closet, in the piano or television set is comparable to those of finding the proverbial needle in the

22

The hamster spends a great deal of its time plotting and figuring out ways to escape. It is only trying to satisfy its natural curiosity. Shown is a longhaired satinized dove male hamster.

haystack. You won't find him by searching, but you can recapture him easily enough. All you need is a carrot, a deep pail with smooth sides (or a smooth metal wastebasket) and a few bricks or blocks of wood. Another hamster (preferably a female if the escapee is a male) will help. So will some of the wood shavings and nest material taken from the hamster cage. This is what you do: First cover all toilets and aquariums, drain the bathtubs and sinks, and put out the cat. Actually, "put out the cat" should be the *first* thing you do. Before you go to bed, set the pail on the floor. Pile the bricks or blocks to form an outside stairway. Rub the carrot up the "steps" and drop it into the pail. Place the wood shavings with the carrot. Put the other caged hamster, if you have one, on the floor alongside the pail. Then go to sleep. In the morning the escaped hamster will be in with the shavings; it happens every time.

It's advisable that the female hamster, if you are using her as bait, be in a small separate cage within the trap. It's for *his* protection; if she's not in a receptive mood she just might kill the poor thing after he falls in.

Hamsters are also fond of pipes, tubes, conduits, tunnels and similar long, dark spaces. You can take advantage of this knowledge by trying a live trap—there are many in the marketplace. Most are tunnel-shaped with one or two doors at the ends and a treadle in the center. They work. Bait the treadle with something sticky—like peanut butter, with some grain pressed into it.

If you have any mice in the house and they get trapped with the hamster, he will probably kill them. But a rat will almost surely kill the hamster, so don't leave the "trap" any longer than necessary if there are any rats around.

Even though escape is almost inevitable, you can try to prevent it. Your hamster is not quite quicksilver, but he can get through any opening as large as his head. He's a tiny animal, and rather than risk a loss you should make sure the cage is as strong and tight as possible, with an outside latch of some sort.

Opposite, above and below: Hamsters are slow eaters. Although they do enjoy soft foods, they are designed and equipped to consume hard materials, such as seeds and nuts, which are slowly chewed and slowly digested.

Bedding for the cage can be nearly anything which is not poisonous, overly aromatic, sharp or entangling. Paper confetti, wood chips, sawdust, shavings, mowed hay, chopped hay, and cotton waste, have all been used successfully.

Feeding

Hamsters are gnawing animals. They are therefore slow eaters; eaters of seeds, nuts and hard foods. Although they do enjoy soft foods, they are designed and equipped to consume hard materials which are slowly chewed and slowly digested. Because of this hamsters are constant nibblers. This also helps to explain the value of the hoarding instinct and the cheek pouches; hamsters just naturally want to forage for food and carry it in their pouches to a hiding place to eat at leisure. If hamsters' food were of a soft, quick-spoiling nature this would not be possible—and soft, quick-spoiling foods are also extremely difficult to *remove* from the pouch; remaining stuck there, they are the source of various health problems.

Whether you feed your pet once a day at a specified time, or you simply replenish the stock for his hoard when it runs low, it is he who will decide when to eat and what to eat. You may sometimes notice that your hamster is eating when he looks half asleep—with his eyes closed or half-closed. It may be that because hamsters under natural conditions do most of their eating underground, eyesight is not important for managing their food.

Just because your hamster accepts what you offer and stuffs it into his pouches, it doesn't mean that he plans to eat it soon, or ever. He just wants it, period. It may be something soft for bedding, or perhaps it is something that only a hamster could want.

The best diet for hamsters is a varied one, although sunflower seeds seem to be their passionate favorite. The diet should contain fresh raw greens, seeds, nuts, milk, fresh raw fruits, meats, vegetable roots and tubers, insects, eggs and prepared pelleted food. Actually, a dry mixture of cracked or whole corn, kibbled dog food, dog biscuits, sunflower seeds, wheat, and peas or beans is hard to beat. Supplement it with small fresh portions of newly mowed clover or hay, vegetables such as carrot, lettuce, potato—the less highly flavored varieties seem to be favored. Given a choice, most hamsters prefer apple over orange, lettuce over cabbage. (But feed the lettuce sparingly because it is a laxative.)

Water is vital but large quantities are not required.

Soft green vegetables and fruits do not lend themselves to pouch-packing and they are often eaten on the spot. They make an excellent diet supplement for hand feeding while you are taming and training your pet.

Hamsters are constant nibblers. They just naturally want to forage for food and carry it in their pouches to a hiding place where they can eat it at their leisure.

The best diet for hamsters is a varied one, although sunflower seeds seem to be their passionate favorite.

Above: Your pets should have a surplus of hard grains such as nuts, seeds, and corn.

Below: soft green vegetables and fruits do not lend themselves to pouch-packing and therefore are often eaten on the spot.

Soft foods should be fed carefully—thoughtfully. As suggested above, the hamster's hoarding-storing system was not really made for such foods.

Most hamster owners feed their pets some sort of pelletized dried vegetable material, available at pet shops. The dried, compressed food is scientifically designed to furnish all the vital substances except water. This is suitable for your hamster's basic diet, but it should be supplemented with some treats—nuts, sunflower seeds, carrots, fruit and meat.

Sharp foods such as whole oats are also thought by some pet owners to be unsafe in the cheek pouch. Fortunately, most unsafe or unwholesome foods will be rejected by your pet and that will be the end of that.

A newborn hamster is nursed by his mother until his fur grows and his eyes open. He should then get soft foods as he is weaned away from his mother's milk. Whole wheat bread soaked in milk is a fine food for baby hamsters and a fine supplemental food for their mothers. Milk sours, and so you should replace this milksop frequently.

Slightly older hamsters, and breeding females, do well if offered supplemental treats like boiled eggs, live crickets, grasshoppers, lean meat, wheat germ, and mixed birdseed (containing millet and rape seed.)

You need not be afraid of offering too much of any food to these pets. Since hamsters will not overeat, you cannot possible overfeed them. What they do not eat they will hide away. All you must remember is to avoid feeding an excess of food which spoils or smells when it gets old.

If you have just one or two animals, your best source of food supply is your pet dealer who has packaged mixtures designed for hamsters. All you need to add is a watering bottle and occasional soft fresh treats like crickets, carrot, apple or a little lettuce. A *little* lettuce.

Of course, if you go in for large scale breeding it will be much cheaper to prepare your own mixes from scratch.

Some specific foods you might include in your hamster's diet are: beets, beet tops, bird seed, sunflower seeds, boiled eggs, carrots and carrot tops, live crickets, grasshoppers, corn, corn bread and cracked corn, dog biscuits, milk, lean meat, nuts, oats, potatoes and wheat germ.

All vegetables and fruits should be fresh, raw and washed. Milk should be pasteurized, condensed or evaporated. Citrus fruits are a controversial item of diet; you might try feeding a bit to your hamster and see how he reacts. (Vitamin C is apparently not required in the hamster's diet.) Cooked meats have also been a con-

Sammy chillin.

Opposite: Slightly older hamsters and breeding females may enjoy a supplement of mixed birdseed containing millet and rape seed (as shown above). Lettuce and leafy greens (below) should be offered sparingly, as too much can cause diarrhea.

28

troversial food for hamsters, with some authorities believing that it induces cannibalism of young by their mothers.. Others, however, disagree. Hamsters sometimes like boiled beef bones to grind their teeth on, and they probably derive some value from the minerals in the bone. Dry pellets and dog biscuits, incidentally, are also considered a good tooth-grinding medium.

Wheat germ oil, or substances containing it, is a good addition to the hamster's diet. Some pet shops sell ripe whole wheat as it comes from the stalk. This is as good a way as any to assure your pet of Vitamin E. Raw peanuts are also a good source of this vitamin.

Water, of course, is needed by the hamster. Much of it is obtained from the soft foods, but if pellets form a major part of your hamster's diet, a plentiful supply of fresh, clean water is an absolute must.

If your watering system is working reliably, you may leave your animals unattended for a weekend with little risk. Hedge your bet with a piece of raw potato or apple for extra moisture and be sure there is a plentiful supply of grain and dog biscuits in the cage. Incidentally, many experienced animal keepers supplement the diets of virtually all domestic and captive mammals with dried dog rations. This can be in biscuit or kibble form. The advantages of dry food are that trace elements are guaranteed available and spoilage is hardly ever a problem.

If, instead, you leave water in a dish in the cage, your hamster may decide that it is just the place to hoard his food or leave his droppings.

HOARDING

Your hamster wants to hoard his food. A female with young is especially active in this hoarding business. A nervous hamster, or one who has been recently moved, or one whose cage has just been cleaned, will stuff his pouches until they look like they will burst.

An adult hamster will keep the hoard in one place in his cage and will try to keep it as far as possible from the spot where he leaves his droppings. Try not to disturb the hoard when you clean the one soiled area in the cage.

Do not change the litter or dispose of the hoarded food more often than once a week, and preferably less often. This is especially important in the case of a female with young. Your sense of smell, at any rate, will be the best guide to how often you have to clean the cage thoroughly. You will find that a hamster cage (or even a hamster colony with thousands of cages) is practically odorless.

After your hamster has fully packed his pouches and carried his prize home he will often use his forepaws to help push the pouches from behind to unload the cargo.

30

Hamsters need an occasional tooth-grinding medium to keep their teeth trim.

Above: A variety of cages from which to choose. Below: Water should always be clean and fresh.

Just because your hamster accepts what you offer and stuffs it into his pouches doesn't mean that he plans to eat it soon, or ever. He just wants it, period. Above is a golden dominant spot female hamster nibbling on something good.

Hamster Diseases

Hamsters live about 1000 days, and with proper care they should never be sick. If your hamster does become sick, treat him with simple, intelligent care.

Let's start out with a few basics and then get into the details. Basic number one is that hamsters are naturally hardy and naturally resistant to disease. Basic number two is that they are subject to the same *sort* of ailments that man is subject to, and for the same reasons. That is: injuries, nutritional diseases, infectious diseases. Basic number three is that hamsters respond to disease cures much as people do. In other words, some hamsters recover with care, some recover spontaneously, and others die regardless, just like people. So much for the basics.

Detail number one is that the homily *"Cleanliness is next to Godliness"* is true. Many diseases can be cured or prevented by using clean bedding and changing it before it becomes an invitation to vermin. Remember to disinfect the cage when you change the bedding. This is easy with glass or metal or plastic cages, but much more difficult with wood. Water bottles should also be kept clean and, of course, your pet should never be expected to drink water which you wouldn't drink.

The second detail is another homily, *"You are what you eat."* Your pets should never get any more soft foods than they will *eat* immediately. *Eat*, not store. Remember the cheek pouches and the hoarding instinct. Soft foods include meat, fruits, vegetables, cooked foods and milk products—everything except grains, kibbled foods, pellets and water. Your pets should have a surplus of hard grains to hoard. This is important for their mental health as well as their physical health. Remember, they forage during the cool night and probably eat from the hoard three cool feet underground during the heat of the day. Nutrition is simple if you let your pet decide. Start with the list in the chapter on feeding and supplement it with small portions of whatever treats your pet enjoys.

The third detail concerns injuries. *Prevent* them. Treat your pet with loving, thoughtful kindness. Don't try to remake him. Don't push him to "higher" things. He is not an acrobat or flier, or even much of a climber. Cage him and handle him with the view in mind that he must never fall. Also cage him so that he cannot escape and so no cat or dog or undisciplined child can get in to abuse him. Really, that's about all that there is.

Now for cures. Let's start with symptoms and then go into diagnoses and treatment.

Hamsters are naturally hardy and naturally resistant to disease. If your hamster does become sick, treat it with simple, intelligent care.

Supplement the basic hamster diet with small portions of whatever treats your pet enjoys.

You can prevent injuries if you handle your hamster with the view in mind that it must never fall. Also, cage the hamster so that it cannot escape and so no cat or dog (or undisciplined child) can get in to abuse it.

Ruffled coat, loss of appetite, wasting, diarrhea, eventual death—this could be *salmonellosis,* an intestinal infection which can become epidemic. It may be transmitted by wild rodents or dirty drinking water or spoiled soft foods. Control and cure require that you destroy all sick animals.

No, it's not being cruel. You're saving the infected hamster from an otherwise lingering, miserable death and you're protecting the other hamsters from contracting the disease.

Isolate the healthy animals, sterilize cages and equipment. Start anew with fresh bedding and a new food supply.

As an isolated disorder, diarrhea is often the result of an overfeeding of soft vegetables and fruits—especially lettuce, as mentioned earlier—or spoiled foods.

Ruffled coat, loss of appetite, rapid breathing, nasal discharge, coughing, sneezing, catarrh. This is an inflammation of the lungs—*pneumonia.* Again, as in salmonellosis, the same measures are suggested. Also, avoid sneezing at your pets; they may catch your cold. These respiratory diseases generally occur in malnourished colonies of damp and/or overcrowded animals.

The symptoms of a *cold* are inactivity and ears held against the head. The hamster's nose may appear swollen because he ruffles his fur when wiping the nasal discharge. In advanced stages he will sniffle and sneeze, get thin, and his fur will lose its luster. As above, treat cold and sniffles with plenty of fresh, wholesome foods, a clean cage, and warm, dry bedding.

Poor general condition, loss of hair, he shakes his head and scratches his ears. Eventually, ears, nose and genitals are covered with gray warty scabs. The diagnosis is mange, caused by parasitic spiders or insects. The control is a high standard of hygiene. Wash your hands after handling each animal. Sterilize all cages and appliances. Replace all bedding. Avoid contact between infected and uninfected animals. There are mange cures available through your veterinarian. He can diagnose mange and possibly he will suggest a bath with benzyl benzoate, dimethyl-thianthrene or gammexane preparations.

Vermin and skin disorders are generally associated with dirty cages. Golden hamsters are desert animals—they don't bathe or swim by choice. But they do keep themselves clean, spending about 20 per cent of their waking hours licking and grooming themselves. They prefer dry quarters and dry fur, and if their cages are clean and dry, with a good supply of nesting litter of shavings, straw, or other dust-free material, they will stay clean and vermin-free.

Maintain high standards of hygiene in order to prevent diseases from spreading. Many diseases can be cured or prevented by using clean bedding and changing it before it becomes an invitation to vermin. The hamster above is a healthy specimen.

There is a fly, much like a housefly, which may deposit its eggs on nursing mothers or baby hamsters. The maggots dig into the hamster's flesh and steal milk. If there are such flies in your area, you should use fine screen on the hamster cage and remove any maggots you find. Fortunately, this species of fly is rare.

Skin parasites are not common on pet hamsters, but if they do infest your colony, you have a problem. Read Chapter Nine entitled "Ectoparasites" in *Breeding Laboratory Animals,* edited by G. Porter and W. Lane-Petter and published by T.F.H. Publications, Inc.

If the symptoms are poor general condition, diarrhea, and wet and dirty hind quarters, your pet has an infection called "wet tail." This is often fatal and can become epidemic. Wet tail is often a disease of neglect. Damp cages, spoiled food and malnourished animals are generally involved. The cure is doubtful—the control is obvious.

A wet tail is also a sign of *constipation.* Constipation in young or adult hamsters is directly related to the amount of pellets and water they have been fed. If you give your hamster pellets, you must provide plenty of fresh water. If you have more than one hamster, make sure that one bossy animal does not take all the water. In case constipation does occur, give youngsters milk-sop and greens; give adults carrots, leafy vegetables and fruit.

Running eyes sometimes indicate trouble in the cheek pouches, which may be stuffed with such food as bread or rolled oats that gets stuck back near the shoulder. Tears then form in the eye on the side where the stuck particle is. If this happens, flush out the pouch with water of the hamster's body temperature, using a syringe. Try to get your pet to *eat* soft foods when they are given, instead of stuffing his pouches with them.

Overgrown teeth should be snipped down with a nail clipper, and your hamster should have a bone to gnaw on.

Overgrown nails may be hereditary. Clip them, but not down to the blood vessel. If you plan to breed hamsters, don't mate any that have overgrown nails.

One form of *paralysis* may result from lack of Vitamin D. Feed wheat germ and wheat germ oil. Other forms of paralysis are the result of lack of exercise. Keep your pet in a roomy cage, with an exercise wheel or some other amusement that will provide activity. Slight paralysis can be cured by such exercise and more fresh foods added to the hamster's diet. There is not much you can do if your pet develops heavy paralysis, so it is wisest to provide the big cage and wheel to prevent it.

Running eyes may be an indication of trouble in the cheek pouches, which may be stuffed with such soft food as bread or rolled oats that gets stuck back near the shoulder.

The hamster leads a short but intense life. Life expectancy is approximately 1000 days.

Infertility is sometimes caused by cold or not enough Vitamin E in the diet. Hamsters that are constantly annoyed, and hamsters that are too fat, may also be infertile. In some recently developed new color strains of hamsters, infertility may be a hereditary weakness.

Stillbirth or death at birth is often the result of falls or rough handling of the mother. Injuries which have gone unnoticed often make normal delivery impossible.

If your hamster has a *tumor, internal bleeding or skin lesions,* the best thing to do is have the vet put him to sleep.

THE OLD HAMSTER

The hamster leads a short but intense life. Any hamster that lives more than 1000 days or about two years and nine months is a rather exceptional specimen. A three-year-old hamster is a rarity.

If your pet suffers from any incurable disease in his old age, you should bring him to your vet for a painless death. You can be sure that the Nembutal, ether or chloroform used will be painless to the animal, and it is far more humane than letting him suffer.

Breeding

If you plan to breed hamsters, you will have an exciting experience. One of the great joys of pet-keeping is having your pets reproduce and watching the young grow to maturity.

Hamsters are noted for their remarkable rate of reproduction. Their period of gestation, sixteen days, is the shortest of any known mammal. The female is in season and receptive to breeding every four days. Litters range from two to fifteen, with eight the usual number of hamster cubs born. Their development is very rapid, and maturity is reached in less than three months. It's even possible to breed a hamster cub one month old although this is not recommended. Weaning is generally at about five weeks, and three to seven days after weaning the female can be bred again. Thus you can see that hamster production can be exceedingly great.

Don't try to remake hamster habits, but rather, adapt your techniques and equipment to suit what they do naturally. Hamsters are tunnel dwellers, they mate in the dark and are born in the dark and develop for several weeks in a dark nest at the end of a winding burrow, possibly eight feet long.

Most surface activity is probably at night. This is when they meet and mate. Since the nest at the end of the burrow is the nursery, the place of safety and food storage, it is defended against all comers. The female in her nest might well kill a visiting male. So, when you mate your animals, place the *female* in the cage of the *male*. The chances of a successful mating without bloodshed are increased.

For breeding purposes you should start with stock of the proper age. Provide the female with a cage containing a nest box and soft, clean nesting material. The nest box can be a compartment in a secluded part of the cage. It need not be much larger than a cigar box (no top is needed). Washed rags, tissue paper and pine wood shavings are all good nesting materials.

You can tell the females are receptive to mating when they are more active than usual. This happens every fourth day, or more properly, every fourth or fifth night. A waxy plug develops in the opening of the vagina and it is discharged at the end of each cycle. The female is receptive to breeding at the beginning of a cycle, that is to say, when there is no discharge. This examination technique may be of value to scientists working on special problems, but for breeders of pet hamsters, it is not recommended simply because there is an easier method.

Opposite: A dark grey satin female and a longhaired lilac male getting to know each other.

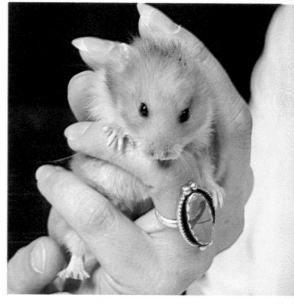

Hamsters are noted for their remarkable rate of reproduction. Their period of gestation, sixteen days, is the shortest of any known mammal.

Opposite: A dove female being approached by a longhaired lilac male.

Sometime after seven p.m. and before eleven p.m., place an active female in the cage of a large experienced male. Within a minute he will have sniffed and begun to mate with her if she is receptive. She will raise her tail and arch her back and stand still. Within thirty minutes they will be done.

Don't leave them together overnight. She will not produce a bigger litter, but she may exhaust or hurt her mate before morning.

They might not hit it off the first time. She may scuffle with him a little; this too is normal even for a receptive female, but if a fight develops, separate them immediately. Then, twenty-four hours later, try again. With this method one male can serve as many as ten breeding females with no strain on him. Remember these simple basic procedures:

Use an experienced male for an inexperienced female.

Try a female for a few minutes and remove her promptly if she is not receptive.

Repeat the routine every night at the same time until she is receptive.

Keep trying the male only until you find a receptive female, then let them mate for thirty minutes.

Once a female begins to mate, clean her cage during those thirty minutes. Fill it with extra bedding and extra food and plan for a litter in two weeks. Leave her strictly alone for nineteen days and nights. If she does not deliver, try the mating technique all over again.

No matter how young your female is, somebody has probably bred one even younger. This is a meaningless exercise in diminishing returns. A female should be fully grown if you are to get any kind of production out of her. Litters from very young females are frequently born dead. If they are too small or too weak they are often killed. This may seem appalling but there is no human-like viciousness involved. Afterwards, the female hamster under *normal* conditions eats her dead or dying young as a sanitary measure.

Plan to breed a female only when she is at least eight or ten weeks old. She will probably be even better if she were twelve weeks old. Try to use an older, experienced male, the first time, anyway.

Keep records. Discard breeders which consistently produce malformed young. Leave pregnant females and females with young strictly alone. Pick up your animals in a box, can, jar or scoop. Don't handle them when transferring animals to cages for mating—your odor may confuse the issue. Avoid picking up the young, especially before their eyes open. If you must pick them

A cinnamon satinized female and a longhaired cinnamon piebald male mating.

up, rub a handful of grain over your hands first. It will tend to mask your odor. The babies photographed for this book were handled without loss, but the females were experienced mothers and the hand-rubbing technique was used.

The young are born blind, naked, helpless. They are about one inch long and weigh 1/14 to 1/8 of an ounce. After about ten days the young begin to move about the cage and nibble soft foods, although they still cannot see. Their eyes open when they are about sixteen days old.

Litters of normal shorthaired hamsters will range from 2 to 15, with an average of 8. Stillbirths, runts and deformities might account for 2%. If your animals have a defect rate of 10%, you ought to find out why. Longhaired hamsters are somewhat harder to produce than normal shorthaired strains. Litters are small and less frequent. Possibly their long hair interferes with mating.

Most female hamsters will produce about six or seven successful litters averaging six or seven cubs per litter in a lifetime. It doesn't seem to matter if you start at age twelve weeks or at twenty weeks for the first litter; a female fizzles out after forty or fifty offspring. If you have a strain which does better, keep them and concentrate on this genetic feature.

PAIR BREEDING

Pair breeding occurs when you simply put a pair together and keep them in the same cage until the female appears pregnant. This technique usually results in a badly abused male. The female will steal his food, scratch and bite him, evict him from his sleeping area, and in extreme cases she may seriously injure or kill him.

In test or pair breeding, if a virgin female receives a preferably experienced male but does not become pregnant, do not give up trying to breed her until a second trial is made. Some virgin hamsters do not become pregnant with the first mating.

COLONY BREEDING

Some commercial breeders use a technique called colony breeding. A large cage is set up with plenty of nesting material, several water bottles, and possibly a few small nest boxes as hiding places. Three full-grown mature males are introduced to the cage. After they become thoroughly accustomed to it—after a day or so—about a half-dozen females are placed in the cage with them. Unless there are really serious fights, the animals are confined together until the females swell up

42

Most female hamsters will produce six or seven successful litters each averaging six or seven cubs per litter. Above is a group of young cream females, both normals and satins.

or until ten or eleven days have passed. They should all be separated by the twelfth day. Don't add any new females until all those in the cage are removed. Then the three males rest a week and another six females are introduced.

The males *must* be permitted to rest at least a week between batches of females, and each female must be placed in a separate cage to bear her young.

Whatever breeding method you use, be sure the female is in her "maternity cage" at least four days before the babies are due. Don't move her until at least three weeks after they are born, and it's better if you wait four or five and the babies are weaned and go their separate ways. Then wait another few weeks before breeding the female again.

Remember that about the time the hamster is weaned, it is sexually mature, and although it is capable of breeding it should not be bred until optimum breeding age is reached. Therefore the sexes should be separated early, before their thirty-fifth day at the longest. They will then weigh about thirty grams (approximately one ounce). A young female, to properly deliver and nurse all her first litter, should weigh at least 100 grams (3⅓ ounces) before she is bred. A fully mature, healthy breeder must weigh 150 to 158 grams (5-5¼ ounces). If you want to be scientific in your breeding work, you should have an accurate scale or balance graduated in quarter-ounces up to eight ounces, or in grams to about 200 grams. Some small postage scales do nicely.

COLOR VARIETIES

The hamster's normal golden color is subject to some slight variation. (See also the later discussion on standards.) Some strains tend to be yellower, others darker. Bellies are sometimes white, gray, yellow-white or blue-white. These differences are slight and are of little interest to the casual hamster keeper. However, the serious breeder can intensify a color trait and eventually create a color which varies enough to be distinctive.

In addition to these slight differences, there are several different, stand-out color strains. The albino hamster has white fur and pink eyes. The trait is recessive. Only a pair of albinos can produce a 100 per cent albino offspring. However, two golden hamsters can produce an albino by the very rare process of mutation. This is the result of a violent genetic change and each time it occurs a new strain of albino could be established. This has already happened several times. Albino offspring can also result from the mating of golden parents if, by a rare coincidence, both parents have recessive albino genes.

If you decide to breed hamsters, aim for rich, dense fur; broad, round bodies; bold eyes; erect, uncreased ears; straight backs; and good dispositions. If you are careful about diet, care, and choice of breeding stock, your results should be very satisfactory.

A ruby-eyed, dark-eared, white young male. The long hair can be easily smoothed with a dry toothbrush.

A group of baby cream and cream-banded hamsters.

These hamsters seem to enjoy gnawing on tree bark.

A pair of longhaired cream satins.

A group of young female hamsters. Left to right: a tortoiseshell, a white-bellied tortoiseshell, a light grey tortoiseshell, and a satinized dominant spot.

Opposite: Mesocrice-tus auratus, *more commonly known as the golden short-haired hamster.*

The above female hamster has fawn coloring.

Opposite: A piebald variety, so named because of the evenly placed white patches throughout the fur.

Another color variation is the "pied," "harlequin," or "panda" hamster. This too is the result of genetic mutation. The markings are variable, with each strain different from other strains, and even individual hamsters vary in coloring from their nestmates. Some are gray-gold mottled on white; others are gold on white, and still other color combinations have been seen.

Pandas tend to be high strung and if you are a beginning hobbyist, you should not choose them as your first pair to breed, since they require more care than the others.

Each color variety—golden, albino, panda—can be bred to each other. The results will not be hybrids, but merely mixed strains. These mixed strains might bring more vigor to a panda or albino line, but to re-establish the recessive color trait, selective inbreeding must be done.

When breeding hamsters, aim for rich, dense fur; broad, round bodies; bold eyes; erect, uncreased ears; straight backs, and good dispositions. If you are careful about diet, care, and choice of breeding stock, your results should be very satisfactory.

Two color varieties: a dominant spot hamster (left) and a piebald (right).

This is a black-eyed white female hamster. If the eyes were pink instead of black, it would be considered an albino.

Standard Features

Hopefully you are reading this book *before* buying your first hamster. If that's not the case, read this chapter anyway, and when you breed your pet, aim for the features established in 1945 by British fanciers when they formed their first hamster club:

"The hamster shall be cobby, well-conditioned in body, with large head, broad skull, and short in face, blunt-nosed, avoiding all rat-like appearance. The head shall be well set in the body, as short necked as possible, with the general outline producing a smooth curve from the tip of the nose to the nape of the neck. The eyes shall be bold and prominent. The ears shall be set well apart, shall be large and of good width and shall be carried extended and alert when the animal is actively awake.

And on and on, with comments on the coloration, size, chest band pattern, belly fur, head markings, shape of ears, etc.

So much for the standard. What it means to a pet keeper might take a little translating. For example, "cobby" means sturdy and thick-set. It is the opposite of slinky. The ideal hamster should be built like a grizzly bear and not like a Norway rat. The head should be as wide between the centers of the ears as from the nose to the top of the skull. The hamster should be large. The larger the better, as long as the other features are not lost.

More recently, standards have been established for the Golden Agouti and the Golden Fawn hamsters, as well as provisional standards for the Panda and Cream hamsters, but the basic frame upon which the hamster hangs his hair is still the same.

Normal Golden Hamster Standard

Type

The hamster shall be cobby, well-conditioned in body, with large head, broad skull, and short in face; blunt-nosed, avoiding all ratlike appearance. The head shall be well-set in the body, as short-necked as possible, with the general outline producing a smooth curve from the nose tip over to nape of the neck. The eyes shall be bold and prominent; ears set well apart, large, and of good width, and carried alert when the animal is actively awake.

20 points

Color

The top color shall be a rich, deep gold, approaching light chestnut, reaching from nose to tail, free from shading, and of black ticking hairs. Top color carried well down the fur, with a uniform blue-gray under-color at the base of the hairs.

40 points

Size

The animal shall be as large as possible, due allowance being made for sex in the mixed classes.

15 points

Here is a fine example of the normal golden hamster. Notice the black cheek flash behind its ear.

Cheek-flash and Crescents

The black cheek-flash shall be clear and deeply pigmented, tapering to a point ending behind the base of each ear; bordered by the rear white crescent, which shall also be clearly defined and as true white as possible. The front white crescent shall be in the form of a short curve up the face.

10 points

Chest Band

The chest band shall be unbroken, well furred, and golden brown in color.

5 points

Belly Fur

The belly fur shall be as nearly white as possible, and of good density.

5 points

Condition

The fur shall be soft, short, dense, and glossy; the animal well-fleshed and sturdy.

5 points

Penalties for All Standards

Disease of complete intractibility—Total Disqualification
Wounds, scars, or damaged ears—Minus 10 points
Dirty staging—Minus 10 points
White hairs on top-coat, face, etc.—Minus 5 points

To the right and below: The hamster loves to stuff its cheek pouches full of food. The pouches hold quite a bit, as you can see. Later, the hamster will use its front paws to push out the food and deposit it in a secret hiding place.

Raising Young Hamsters

Hamsters have raised hamsters for centuries with no help from us. If we insist on helping, we must do it passively. Provide the female with plenty of bedding, privacy and ample food for hoarding and eating. The water supply must be available to the babies even when their eyes are barely open. Many young hamsters die of thirst when they are weaned, because the water bottle tube is so high that they cannot reach it.

Soft foods, bread and milk, lettuce, meat, hard-boiled eggs are all good for babies—they will eat soft, moist bread three or four days before their eyes are fully open. They will even pack their tiny cheek pouches while their eyes are not open.

Don't help the mother gather her new litter as they are born. She will do it by herself after the last cub arrives. Keep the cages cool, dry, out of drafts, free from spoiling food, and protected from vermin, dogs, cats and little children. Keep the cage out of direct sunlight.

The babies should be sexed and separated after they stop nursing so that they cannot breed while too young. They might try when only four weeks old, but here is the time when you should make your presence felt.

If the mother kills her babies, it may be because you made her nervous or did not adequately shield her from some other irritant. If the mother eats her babies, it may be because she and they are undernourished, *i.e.,* underfed. If she kills them but does not eat them, it may

Don't help the mother gather her new litter as they are born. She will do it by herself after the last cub arrives.

These baby hamsters are only thirty minutes old. Hamsters are born naked (without fur) and blind.

be because she is poorly nourished, *i.e.,* lacking a mineral or a vitamin.

Young females who fail with their first litter often mature to become steady heavy producers of high quality young. The best productivity seems to come from females after their first litter but before they're too old.

Hamsters are expected to live only 1000 days, and with a four day rhythm for ovulation and a two week period of gestation, the hamster has a short, intense life. If you want production, you must utilize their time efficiently. Don't let them waste it in hibernation, estivation or malnutrition.

When you raise young hamsters, give them room to grow, fresh food—including greens and animal protein—convenient clean water and cool dry bedding. The emphasis on cool is because an overly warm hamster will estivate—go into a deep, sleep-like hibernation which is so deep you might well assume your animal is dead and dispose of him. This estivation is nature's way of carrying a furry animal over a hot period in a dry desert environment. How hot? Over 80°F. is estivating temperature. Nights are cool, the hamster needs fur for his evening outdoor activity, but the hot, dry midday or hot, dry season with no rain and no juicy fruits for liquid, will induce estivation. To get your animal out of this state, circulate cool air and reduce the light.

When you raise hamsters in cool or cold places, they may hibernate. Same idea. To bring back activity, raise the temperature above 50°F. but below 70°F., and increase the amount of light, especially sunlight, if possible.

As you raise your hamsters, you may want to keep track of their growth. Use a 500 gram capacity beam balance and a scoop or small cardboard box to load the animal onto the balance. If the scoop has a round-number weight, say 50 or 100 grams, subtraction will be easier. A full-grown normal golden short-haired hamster will weigh about 150 grams. One outstanding feature of the longhaired hamster is his size—that is, *apparent* size, because of all that hair. Practically everyone who sees or handles them is bound to remark on their great size and weight. Here is where the scale is useful.

At the end of 1000 days of raising your hamster, he may be cancerous, mangy, rheumatic, or just too decrepit to even eat properly. Take him to your veterinarian and have him humanely and painlessly put to sleep.

Opposite: As you raise your hamsters, you may want to keep track of their growth. These baby black hamsters are twelve days old.

Opposite: The hamsters' eyes are just starting to open at twelve days old.

Hints From A Professional

Scattered over the country are several hundred professional hamster breeders. The author visited a typical small establishment and discussed some of the special problems of hamster production with the proprietor of Rocky Hill Farms in Monsey, New York, Mr. William Lees.

Also present was Mr. Joseph Stocker, of Ramsey, New Jersey. Mr. Stocker is a laboratory animal jobber. As a jobber he performs the important function of assuring a fluctuating market of a steady supply. Schools and some university laboratories shut down in the summer, and other organizations performing research also vary their requirements either seasonally or according to their research programs. Mr. Stocker anticipates these needs and arranges with breeders to have stock of certain size available to meet the demand.

Mr. Lees has several buildings on his property, where he raises mice and hamsters. The greatest part of his production, typically, is for research. This calls for normal golden hamsters. The other color varieties are almost completely limited to the demands of the pet trade.

Mr. Lees keeps his hamster colony in a building which is heated in the winter. It's well insulated not only for winter warmth but also for summer coolness. If the building were cold in winter the hamsters would hibernate and there would be no production. Warm weather also makes hamsters sleepy, and very warm temperature brings on a condition of deep sleep which is much like winter hibernation. The animals are then so limp and

The good treatment that is received by hamsters cared for by a conscientious keeper is evidenced by the hamster's appearance and behavior.

A female cream protects her eleven-day-old litter. Remember not to disturb the newborn hamsters nor the mother until after the weaning period.

quiet that they actually appear at first glance to be dead. The Syrian climate is hot during the day, but then the hamster is asleep, deep in its burrow. At night when it is cool the hamster comes out to forage for grain and greens. Thus you see that it's normal for your pet to sleep during the day. If it sleeps "like the dead" day and night, you might try to find a more temperate place for its cage.

Mr. Lees suggested that if a pet keeper has a problem with a female who eats her young he should suspect that she is suffering from a diet deficiency, probably a lack of calcium and protein. Feed her milk, dog biscuits, and fresh or dried peas and beans.

If she smothers, deserts or otherwise kills her young but does not eat them, Mr. Lees suggests that she probably did this out of nervousness. This often happens if she feels insecure through lack of adequate bedding, lack of privacy from humans and other hamsters or lack of milk to feed her babies. First litters from young or undernourished mothers are sometimes killed, but after adequate rest and feeding the same female will produce large healthy litters and raise them to maturity with no trouble.

Mr. Lees keeps his hamsters in screened wooden cages. Water comes from the standard bottle-and-tube arrangement. Bedding and nest material is pine wood shavings. Food includes animal pellets supplemented with grain and raw fresh clean vegetables.

One rule Mr. Lees suggests concerning vegetables is to feed your hamster only what you would serve on your own table. Do not use wilted, dirty or stale vegetables. Diarrhea is only one of several diseases a hamster may get from second quality greens.

Another hint from Mr. Lees concerns the feeding of soft or sticky foods. White bread and rolled oats not only are lacking in nutrition, but, if they are picked up by a hamster and stuffed into the pouches, may get stuck, sometimes back near the shoulder, and cause the eyes to tear. "Prepared" foods like cake, bread, crackers, meal and rolled oats are not part of the natural adult hamster diet and should not be hoarded in the pouches. By contrast a sunflower seed or grain of dry corn or wheat is smooth and slippery and can be easily pushed out of the pouch when the hamster is ready to hide it or to eat it.

Some of the points Mr. Lees and Mr. Stocker brought up were not primarily concerned with commercial production but are rather tricks and techniques which any pet keeper should know about, and they deserve credit for passing on "trade secrets" which bear so directly on their livelihood.

Opposite: Raising hamsters can be fun as well as profitable.

Mr. Lees recommends pine wood shavings as bedding and nest material. Cedar chips work well also.

Opposite: A Chinese hamster.

Hamsters in Research

Hamsters have proved valuable in research for several reasons. They are easy to keep, easy to breed and easy to infect with human diseases. They respond to many diseases in the same way humans do, and they can often be cured with the same drugs. This makes them wonderful research tools. They have been used at one time or another for studies of bomb radiation, tooth decay, reproduction, hormones, influenza, tuberculosis, leprosy, diet and cancer.

Because of the increasing importance of hamsters in the world of science, the National Research Council has proposed a set of standards for laboratories to follow in the breeding, care and management of Syrian hamsters. Those standards follow in abridged form.

HAMSTERS AS RESEARCH ANIMALS

The Syrian hamster, *Mesocricetus auratus,* has had a relatively short history as an experimental animal. Descendants of the original groups that were captured in Syria in 1930 were subsequently brought to England and still later to the United States. This species is being used extensively in infectious and parasitic disease investigation, vascular studies, nutrition research, dental research, the study of compounds that demonstrate estrogenic activity, and studies that involve observations concerning tumors.

In research, it is of great importance that the animal material used be as uniform and standardized as possible in order to obtain repeatable results within a laboratory or between laboratories. Uniformity of biological material likewise increases the accuracy of results and improves the efficiency of research by decreasing the number of repetitive experiments required to ascertain that a particular result is not due to chance.

As with other laboratory animals, genetic and environmental factors, acting separately or concurrently, contribute to biological variability in the hamster. Thus, to increase uniformity, controls must be applied to both. The control of genetic variability can be accomplished to a considerable extent by the rigid application of a particular mating system(s) and selection pressures, depending on how much uniformity is required and the particular characteristic(s) involved. The important fact to keep in mind is that genetic uniformity is possible (even though individual variation within a population is evident) if the mating system and selection criteria initially established are consistently followed. The control of environmental factors, likewise, can be

Is this longhaired dark grey satin hamster camera shy, or is it just absorbed in shelling a seed it's found?

accomplished to a considerable extent by the establishment of, and adherence to, uniform and optimal conditions and procedures in colony management. Strict controls of cleanliness, nutrition, temperature and humidity, and disease prevention, for example, will promote the development of environmental uniformity, thus contributing to the over-all uniformity of the animals.

Though both genetic and environmental uniformity are difficult to obtain, the judicious application of current knowledge and experience will permit much progress to be made. The standards presented are the result of this knowledge and experience.

GENERAL CONSIDERATIONS

The facilities, equipment, and husbandry procedures shall be designed and operated to afford maximum environmental control, optimal comfort and welfare for the animals, and minimal opportunity for the transmission of diseases and parasites from one animal to another and from group to group. The physical facilities shall be designed and constructed so that clean and soiled material and equipment will be maintained separately and shall afford maximum control of temperature, humidity, and light, so that the animals shall have optimal conditions for their comfort and welfare. The caging equipment and feeding and watering devices used shall be designed and fabricated so as to afford maximum comfort and welfare for the animals, minimum opportunity for the transmissions of diseases and parasites, and ease and efficiency of sanitizing and sterilizing. Auxiliary equipment such as washing machines, cage racks, rolling equipment (dollies, tables, carts, etc.), and fixed equipment (cabinets, sink, etc.) shall be designed and fabricated according to the best available knowledge and shall be used in such manner as to promote maximum environmental control and efficiency in operation.

Operating procedures shall be performed according to the recommendations of these standards and shall consist of those practices that will include the best information and experience in nutrition, genetics and animal breeding, care and maintenance, colony management, disease control, etc., so that maximum environmental control is accomplished and optimal conditions for the comfort and welfare of the animals are provided.

For the purposes of these standards, sanitization and sterilization are defined as follows:

Sanitization—to make physically clean and to remove or destroy agents injurious to the health of laboratory animals.

Sterilization—the act or process of killing all living cells, especially microorganisms.

Opposite: Both the top and bottom photos portray a red-eyed cream satinized rex angora.

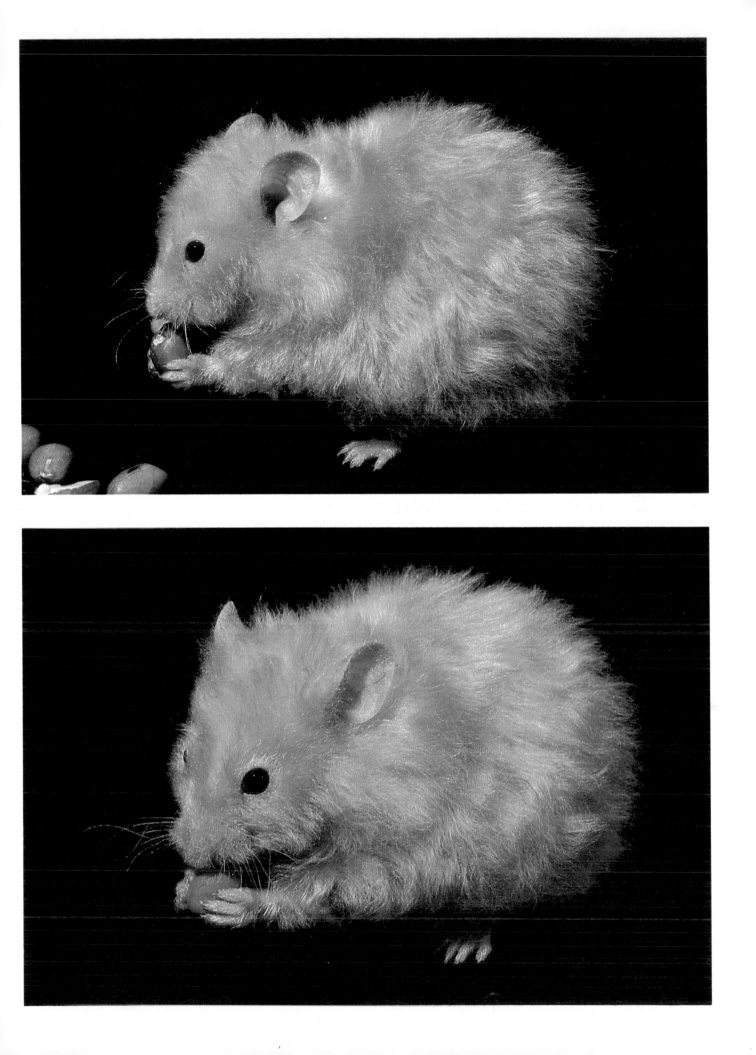

CONSTRUCTION OF FACILITIES

Exterior walls shall be of masonry or metal. Wooden construction other than studding, plates, laths, etc., will not be acceptable. The outside and inside surfaces of these walls shall be rendered impervious to liquids and moisture and be rodent- and vermin-proof. The inside surfaces may be covered with coatings or sheetings that are smooth and hard without pitting and/or cracking and are easily cleaned. All welded, caulked, and mortared joints shall be completely filled.

Interior walls (interior bearing walls and partitions) may be of masonry, metal, masonite, fiberboard, flexboard, transite, drywall, cement plaster, or comparable material, provided that the finished surfaces comply with the specifications noted above for the inside surfaces of the exterior bearing walls. Wooden studding is acceptable for interior walls and partitions.

Roofs may be constructed of any of the materials that are commonly used for this purpose by the building trades. Roof trusses, ridge pole (ridge piece, ridge plate), wall plates, tie beams, king posts, struts, pole plates, and rafters may be of wood. Ceilings shall be used, and constructed of materials equal to those suggested for walls and partitions, and shall be subject to identical finishing conditions. Access panels in ceilings shall completely fill the opening when in a closed position.

New floors shall be constructed of dense mix concrete or equivalent with a smooth surface, coated with a sealer to render them impervious to liquids and moisture, to prevent dusting, and for easy cleaning. A waterproof membrane is recommended. Floors constructed of wood may be used provided that they are completely covered with metal, linoleum, tile, etc. If metal is used, it shall be corrosion-resistant and fastened to the wood without buckling or warping. It shall present a smooth and unbroken surface, and all joints, including those at the walls, shall be closed. If linoleum or tile is used, it shall be firmly affixed to the floor with a suitable moisture- and liquid-resistant adhesive. The upper finished surface shall be smooth and unbroken, and all joints shall be completely filled.

Doors shall be provided for all rooms. These doors shall be so located as to allow entrance and exit to clean and dirty areas. There shall be no intercommunicating doors between rooms. Each door shall have an adequate door latch and lock and shall be rodent- and vermin-proof when in closed position. Door frames shall be sealed to the walls and partitions with caulking or similar material.

A clean environment, proper nutrition, temperature and humidity control, and disease prevention are all important factors which contribute to your hamster's healthy life.

Outside windows are not desirable. It is suggested that a viewing port of transparent glass be installed for inspection purposes. Lights shall be of a type and in a location that simplifies cleaning. If ultra-violet lights are used, they should be of a design that limits the production of ozone below toxic levels.

AIR CONDITIONING

Air conditioning in animal quarters is required. Recirculated air can be used if the system is provided with equipment that can remove and/or destroy all microorganisms, but recirculation is not recommended. Animal room temperatures shall be maintained between 69° and 75° F. It is recommended that 69° to 71° be used for adults and young hamsters in holding rooms, and 72° to 74° for breeding rooms. Relative humidity levels should be maintained between 40% and 60%. Each room shall be provided with air conditioning and humidity controls. It is recommended that graphic recorders be used for tabulations of 24-hour system performance.

Duct work preferably should be located above the ceiling or mounted flush. However, if installed below the ceiling, the upper surface of the duct work shall be sealed to the ceiling or suspended at least six inches below the ceiling to facilitate cleaning. The diffusers and exhaust openings shall be so located and controlled as to avoid drafts. Openings in ventilation grillwork shall not be of a size that will permit the entrance of rodents.

The supply of air shall be such as to provide a minimum of six air changes per hour. The air pressure within clean spaces shall be greater than that in public and refuse areas. Circulating fans may be used during periods of air conditioning system breakdown, repairs, etc. Supplemental exhaust fans, if used, shall be permanently mounted in external window or wall openings and screened. Their frame shall be sealed to the building structure. Standby generators should be available in the event of power failure. Central heating, if used, should be compatible with the requirements stated above.

Water bottles should be used; they should be formed of clear glass and preferably not over one-half pint in capacity.

EQUIPMENT

Cages shall be fabricated of a smooth, corrosion-resistant material. It shall be impervious to liquids and moisture and easily sanitized and/or sterilized. Materials that are considered acceptable include plastics, galvanized metal, stainless steel or other stainless metal alloys, glass, aluminum (hard alloys), and magnesium. Wood is not acceptable. The painting of cages and racks is not recommended. All cages shall have water-tight seams. Fabrication methods used shall be performed in a manner that shall not create crevices. All cages shall have a lid (cover) to prevent the escape of caged animals and the entrance of stray animals. The minimum cage area for a nursing female, including a litter of any size, shall be 150 square inches, and the minimum depth of the cage shall be not less than six inches. The following table lists the allowable floor space per hamster according to age groupings:

Age	Square inches per animal
Weaning to 5 weeks	10.0 or more
5 weeks to 3 months	12.5 or more
Over 3 months	15.0 or more

Racks (stands) shall be fabricated of a smooth, corrosion-resistant material. It shall be impervious to liquids and moisture and easily cleaned, sanitized, and sterilized. If racks are fabricated of pipe or tubular material, all openings shall be closed without crevices. Racks may be of fixed or portable design, arranged to facilitate cleaning activities. Wood is not acceptable.

Food hoppers, if used, shall be constructed of any durable material other than wood, shall be resistant to the gnawing of rodents, and shall be corrosion-resistant when exposed to acids, alkalis, detergents, moisture, liquids, and excreta. They shall be easily sanitized and/or sterilized. The food hopper shall be suspended in a manner that allows at least one inch of clear space between the lower surface of the food hopper and the upper surface of the bedding. The food hopper may be hung from the edge of the cage or from the cage lid, formed as part of the cage lid, or inserted through and supported by the cage lid.

Water bottles shall be used; they should be formed of clear glass and preferably not over one-half pint in capacity. They shall be mounted or suspended in a manner that will prohibit contact by the caged animals. If drinking tubes are used, the tube shall be of corrosion-resistant and durable material. Aluminum, copper, and alloys containing copper are not recommended. Perforated bottle caps that are used in lieu of a combination of stopper and tube are acceptable.

A mechanical cage washer should be used by producers and users. It should be of a design that will ensure a continuous supply of hot water at 180° F. for all phases of the washing and rinsing cycle. The duration of the complete cycle shall not be less than three minutes. There should be at least one rinse after the articles have been washed with a detergent solution. If only one rinse

Food hoppers, if used, should be constructed of any durable material that is resistant to the gnawing of rodents.

is used, it shall be supplied directly from the fresh hot water supply line. The washing machine shall be equipped with pump pressure gauges and a thermometer for each phase of the cycle. It is recommended that the washing machine be equipped with an automatic detergent dispenser and a temperature control.

Each room shall have a small sink primarily for the washing of hands. It should not be used for any other washing purpose. The sink shall be supplied with hot and cold water; dispensers for soap, detergent, and bactericide, separately or as combinations; and a paper towel dispenser. Cabinets, work benches, and carts, *if required*, shall be so located as to facilitate cleaning. It is recommended that these pieces of equipment be portable. Equipment and material not in constant use, or which will not be required in the immediate future, shall not be stored in any animal room.

FOOD AND BEDDING

Food and bedding are two items of expendable material that are purchased by producers and users. Both are generally used in animal facilities without prior treatment and hence are potential sources of contamination for diseases, parasites, and abnormal hormonal stimulation. It is, therefore, urged that producers and users be aware of these problems and exercise care in their purchase and storage.

Food:

The production colony management should obtain the vendor's assurance, and if possible receive guarantees, that the pelleted feed he uses is:
   (a) Within normal acceptable limits of naturally occurring hormone activity.
   (b) Free of additives containing drugs, hormones, or antibiotics.
   (c) Examined for the presence of *Salmonella*.
   (d) Free from rodent and vermin contaminations.
Feed should not be accepted by the production colony management unless it is delivered in clean and sealed containers made of new material. Feed received shall not be accepted unless it is marked with the milling date. Feed older than six weeks from date of milling shall not be fed to the animals. The milling date should be plainly printed on the bag, preferably not in code. Feed shall be stored in a clean, dry, rodent- and vermin-free area in covered containers with tightly fitting lids or in their original sealed containers.

Pelleted food shall be supplied, preferably, on a daily basis. Under no circumstances shall any cage be provided with more than one week's supply of these prepared

Food should be clean, fresh, and in sealed containers.

72

Food supplements should be offered in limited quantities and may be placed on the bedding of the cage for immediate consumption.

foods except during the early lactational period. Pelleted food that is present in food hoppers or cages when cages are scheduled for washing shall be discarded.

Feed supplements, in the form of kale, carrots, apples, etc., if used, shall be washed well. This food should be offered in limited quantities and may be placed on the bedding for immediate consumption. Supplemental food that is left over from the previous day's feeding shall be removed daily.

Bedding

It is recommended that bedding shall be of a composition that is not readily eaten by the animals. It shall not contain substances which are injurious when ingested. Resinous woods and hardwoods are not recommended. White pine coarse sawdust and shavings are recommended. Cedar, basswood, poplar, and crushed corn cobs are acceptable.

Bedding should not be purchased from a source whose storage facilities are not adequately protected from vermin and rodent contamination.

Bedding shall be obtained from the vendor in a container which is non-returnable. If obtained in bags, they shall be non-porous and sealed (i.e., burlap bags shall not be used). Baled bedding shall be obtained in closed containers, i.e., paper or plastic bags, paper wrappings, etc. The bedding shall not contain more than 12-15% moisture when received. The bedding shall be stored in dry, rodent- and vermin-proof, frequently sanitized containers or storage areas.

COLONY OPERATIONS

Procedures in the operation of a colony are of utmost importance, for they determine the extent of the environmental control exercised. The latest designs in physical facilities and equipment are no better than the procedures used in operating them. It is, therefore, strongly recommended that producers and users alike constantly review (and revise) their operating procedures so that optimal conditions of care and management are provided for the animals.

Cleaning

Floors shall be swept and cages and racks dusted at least once each day. The completion of the day's activities should include a complete dusting and sweeping. The use of counter and radiator brushes is acceptable for dusting activities; however, moistened sponges are preferred. Equipment on casters shall be moved for sweeping purposes. Pushbrooms are preferred for they do not create as much dust as straw brooms. The use of sweeping compounds or moistened sawdust is recommended. Floors shall be washed at least once a week with a solution containing a detergent and a bactericide. Walls, ceilings, view ports, doors, etc., shall be washed at least once every three months with a solution containing a detergent and a bactericide. Equipment other than animal cages and racks shall be dusted daily and washed with a solution containing a detergent and a bactericide at least once every three months.

Soiled bedding shall be removed and replenished in the cages at least twice per week. The water supply in each bottle shall be replenished as necessary, preferably on a daily basis. Left over water shall be removed from the bottle prior to refilling. If bottles are not washed, they shall be returned to the cage from which they were removed. It is recommended that water bottles be filled by an automatic bottle filler or by means of a hose mounted on a spring loaded reel and a self-closing faucet. The nozzle of the faucet shall be so designed that it cannot be inserted into the bottle.

Animal cages and racks shall be washed at least once every two weeks. At least once per week is recommended. Water bottles, bottle stoppers, drinking tubes, and food hoppers should be washed at least once each week in an effective cage washing machine. It is recommended that water bottles, stoppers, and tubes be washed daily.

All refuse and cage cleanings shall be placed in metal or plastic containers with closely fitting lids or whose tops can be fastened securely. Acceptable kinds of containers include metal cans, plastic cans, plastic or five-ply paper bags, non-reusable cartons, etc. Uncovered tubs, burlap sacks, baskets, etc., are not acceptable for this purpose. Reusable containers for refuse shall be sanitized after they have been emptied. Partially filled containers shall not be held over until the following day. Refuse containers that are positioned outside of the building and are filled via a chute shall be sanitized after they have been emptied, at the end of the working day. Refuse chutes shall be sanitized at the end of the working day. The incineration of dead animals, refuse, soiled bedding, and used disposable containers is strongly recommended.

Treats such as this should be fastened to the cage so that the hamster has easy access to them.

74

Animal cages and racks should be washed at least once every two weeks.

DISEASE AND PARASITE CONTROL

All new breeding stock and new acquisitions shall be quarantined for a period of at least two weeks in a separate building or in a special room that is not associated with a production colony. A holding room or an animal experimental room is not acceptable. During this period suitable laboratory observations shall be made. It is recommended that newly acquired breeding stock be quarantined and observed through the second filial generation. These observations should include necropsies of all members of preceding generations, especially the retired breeding animals.

Personnel assigned to quarantine areas should not work in other animal rooms, and vice versa. If the above arrangement is not practical, it is recommended that the quarantine areas be serviced after all chores have been completed in the other animal rooms. All persons entering the animal area should shower, or in any case wash themselves thoroughly, and dress in clean outer clothing and special shoes or shoe covers. The clothing and shoes or shoe covers shall be worn only in the assigned work area and shall not be removed from this area except for cleaning. Sanitization of these articles shall be performed at least once each week.

Dead animals shall be removed immediately as detected and placed in proper containers. All sick animals (other than those concerned with research) shall be removed when detected and sacrificed immediately in a humane manner. It is recommended that the daily caretaking routines be so arranged that the animals will be observed at least two times daily. Wherever possible, all dead animals and all the sick which have been sacrificed should be examined daily and necropsies performed. Necessary diagnostic procedures should then be carried out by trained personnel.

Hands shall be washed with soap and a bactericide after sick and dead animals have been handled, even though forceps or other devices are used in the process. If non-disposable devices are used for this process, they shall be sanitized after use in one cage and before they are used in another.

Periodic examinations of samples of hamsters, taken from a representative sample of the cages in the entire production colony (including holding rooms), shall be made by a competent diagnostic laboratory. These samples shall be submitted once each month. The examinations will include tests for the presence of *Salmonella,* enteritis ("wet tail") and endo- and ectoparasites.

An effective vermin and rodent control program shall be maintained. Pets shall not be allowed in or near the animal rooms.

75

All hamsters shall be shipped from colonies in non-returnable containers. These containers shall be made of new material and shall be assembled, stored, and filled in clean quarters that are separate from the animal rooms. Hamsters shall not be returned to a production colony once they have been removed.

Undeclared antibiotics and other drugs may not be used in a production colony.

Visitors shall not be allowed in any animal room, quarantine area, or in any space that is considered to be a clean area unless they wash themselves thoroughly and don approved coverings (hair, body, and feet) before entering an animal room. The number of visitors should be severely restricted.

RECORD KEEPING

Proper records shall be kept by the production colony management in order to (1) determine the efficiency of the operation, (2) trace the origin and spread of diseases, and (3) determine biological performance. It is recommended that users of hamsters maintain mortality records and other pertinent data for animals in holding and quarantine rooms; such data will be of value in determining the efficacy of quarantine procedures and will permit them to relate their animals to the originating colony.

Producers shall maintain records for each cage. The following record forms are recommended:

#1 - Record of Breeding Females

Date of Birth of ♀   ♀ No. _____   Parents: Father _____ Mother _____

Mated to ♂ No.	Litter No.	Date Mated	Date Litter Born	Date Litter Weaned	No. Young Born	No. Young Died	No. Young Weaned	♂♂ Weaned	♀♀ Weaned	Unproductive Matings	Remarks

#2 - Record of Breeding Males

Date of Birth of ♂   ♂ No. _____   Parents: Father _____ Mother _____

Mated to ♀ No.	Date Mated	No. Young Born	No. Young Weaned	Unproductive Matings	Remarks

#3 - Summary Sheet

Date	No. Young Died	No. Litters Eaten	Dead Mothers	Dead Litters	Dead Mothers & Litters	Litters Destroyed	Litters Weaned	Young Weaned	Litter Avge.

Adequate records of performance tests conducted at frequent intervals on a representative sample of the breeding colony shall be maintained to assure the retention of desired traits.

Weaning weight records and weight curves of males and females up to twelve weeks of age shall be made available to users by producers. The weight curves shall be re-determined at least once annually, and these determinations shall be based upon the random selection of complete litters of various sizes, with a minimum of 50 animals of each sex in each determination.

Hamster chews are always a welcomed treat.